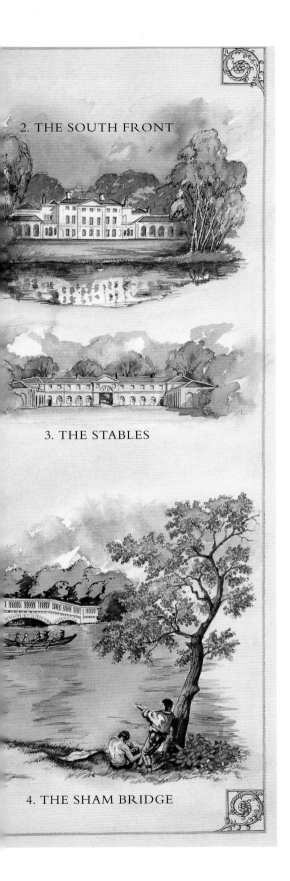

2. THE SOUTH FRONT

3. THE STABLES

4. THE SHAM BRIDGE

Introduction

Kenwood is home to the finest collection of Old Master paintings given to the British nation in the twentieth century. In this Georgian villa you will discover masterpieces by Rembrandt, Vermeer, Hals, Van Dyck, Gainsborough, Reynolds, Turner and many other great artists in a collection formed around 1890 by Edward Cecil Guinness, first Earl of Iveagh, chairman of the world's most successful brewery.

No art collection in London enjoys a more idyllic setting. The architect Robert Adam remodelled and extended an existing house to create a villa in the neoclassical style from 1764 to 1779 for the greatest English judge of the eighteenth century, William Murray, first Earl of Mansfield. Today Kenwood stands in 112 acres (45ha) of gardens and ancient woodland commanding fine prospects towards the centre of London. As Adam himself wrote: 'The whole scene is amazingly gay, magnificent, beautiful and picturesque … nor is it easy to imagine a situation more striking without, or more agreeably retired and peaceful within'. The pastoral landscape of the eighteenth century was transformed by Humphry Repton for the second Earl of Mansfield from 1793.

In 1922 the contents of Kenwood were sold at auction. Lord Iveagh purchased the house in 1925 but died before hanging his paintings here. Since the house opened to the public in 1928 some of the original contents have been tracked down and returned, while a collection of furniture designed by Adam for other houses has been formed to complement the paintings and interiors.

This guidebook provides visitors with a tour of the house and introduces some of the highlights of the collection. It also tells the colourful history of the villa, with its generations of residents, including a future prime minister, a Lord Chief Justice, a Russian Grand Duke and an American millionairess.

The Entrance Front

The origins of the house date back to 1616 when the estate was purchased by John Bill, who later became the King's Printer. The present house dates from around 1700. In the 1760s Robert Adam (1728–92) modified this brick building for his patron William Murray, first Earl of Mansfield (1705–93), the Lord Chief Justice, by extending and rendering the house and adding the portico. Today Kenwood stands in rural surroundings enclosed by woodland, but in the late eighteenth century it enjoyed a more conspicuous setting. Rising the full height of the façade, the imposing classical portico was meant to be seen across the forecourt from Hampstead Lane and from Prospect Hill beyond. Thirty years later David Murray, second Earl of Mansfield (1727–96) commissioned a scheme to improve the grounds from the landscape architect Humphry Repton (1752–1818). As a first step, he diverted Hampstead Lane to the north of Prospect Hill and created the serpentine drive along which today's visitors approach the house.

The North Front of Caen Wood; *engraving by James Heath after Conrad Metz, 1788, showing the forecourt, former entrance gates and the entrance façade as remodelled by Robert Adam, before the brick wings were added in 1793*

ABOVE *The entrance hall*

The Hall

After the grandeur of the portico and forecourt the entrance hall may seem relatively modest, particularly when compared with Adam's entrance halls at Syon (Brentford), Kedleston (Derbyshire) or Harewood (Yorkshire). The main reason for this contrast in scale is that Kenwood was not a great country house, the principal seat of a landed dynasty, but rather the suburban villa of a self-made lawyer who worked in London. A portrait of Robert Adam's patron, when he was plain William Murray (see page 23), hangs in the hall.

Adam gave an illusion of greater height to the ceiling by specifying a low chair rail and low white benches. The benches you see today are not the originals (which were sold at the Kenwood auction in 1922) but were designed by Adam for Bowood House, Wiltshire in 1768.

OPPOSITE *The south front*

The entrance hall ceiling painting by Antonio Zucchi shows Bacchus and Ceres, the Greek gods of wine and agriculture

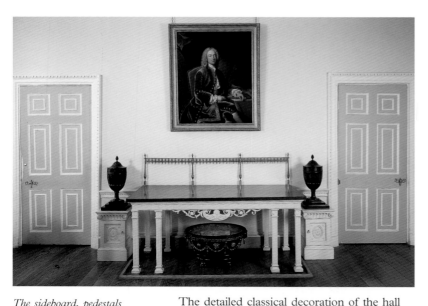

The sideboard, pedestals and wine cooler designed by Robert Adam for Kenwood and made by Sefferin Nelson in 1773 were sold in 1922 but have returned from various private collections

RIGHT *The Great Stairs*

The same four pieces of furniture, as illustrated in an engraving in the Kenwood section of Adam's Works in Architecture (1774)

The detailed classical decoration of the hall reveals the relatively compact way of life in a villa as opposed to a great country house, for in the first Earl of Mansfield's time the entrance hall also served as the formal dining room. Whereas traditionally halls were hung with arms and armour to demonstrate the military power of the host, or with paintings of ancestors and hunting subjects, here there are allusions to Bacchus, the god of wine: in the marble chimneypiece carved by George Burns, in the ornaments of the ceiling by Joseph Rose, in the ceiling paintings of dancing bacchantes (Bacchus worshippers) by Antonio Zucchi (1726–96), and in the central scene of Bacchus with Ceres, the Greek goddess of agriculture.

At this time dining tables were not the permanent standing fixture that they became in the nineteenth century. Rather, they were brought in and assembled from folding tables kept in the stairwells and back passages. Mansfield's guests would have passed through the hall and been received in his Great Room; after the last guest had left the hall it would have been set for dinner.

The ceiling paintings by Zucchi were originally complemented by an overmantel by the same artist representing Diana, goddess of hunting, with her nymphs and hounds. In its place today is a portrait of Edward Cecil Guinness,

first Earl of Iveagh (1847–1927), who bequeathed Kenwood, his collection and the estate to the nation on his death (see page 34).

The dispersal of Kenwood's contents at auction in 1922 and the arrival of Lord Iveagh's collection in 1928 makes it impossible to present Kenwood as if it were still the home of the Mansfield family. However, in 1996 the entrance hall was redecorated by English Heritage to its 1773 colour scheme so that it may now be appreciated as the first in a sequence of rooms that form Lord Mansfield's late eighteenth-century reception suite, culminating in his Great Room.

Take the door to the right of the sideboard to proceed along the route created for the first Earl of Mansfield's guests.

The Great Stairs

Before Adam built the Great Room or Library on the ground floor the principal reception room in the house would have been the Upper Hall, directly above the entrance hall.

In the morning Lord Mansfield could have used these stairs to descend from his bedroom and enter the Breakfast Room via the door beyond the stairs, or his Dressing Room through an adjacent door. Originally the stairs were lit by a window in the far wall of the landing; this was blocked when the second Earl

added the north wings between 1793 and 1796. At the same time a ceiling designed by Adam was destroyed to admit the present skylight.

The room is usually hung with portraits of Lord Mansfield and his future wife (see page 24). There is no evidence of large paintings being hung on the upper level of the stairwell; the empty frames are simply fixed architectural mouldings to break up the empty walls. The first Earl of Mansfield did not collect paintings, but was a great bibliophile.

The Ante Chamber

As you step into the Ante Chamber, you enter the wing added to the older house by Adam between 1767 and 1770. Here you can admire his ingenuity as an architect of the picturesque (see page 26). Following Adam's reception route you have experienced a series of contrasts in space, light and colour, from the tall white portico to the low ceiling of the blue, purple, green and white entrance hall, to the Great Stairs in a room rising the full height of the house, with an inviting vista into a colonnade.

Stepping through the short passage, you might expect to continue through the single door directly opposite. In Adam's day the double doors on the left did not exist; instead, the solid north wall contained a statue in a niche. You notice that the colonnade is only a screen comprising two columns and two pilasters; the closed door at the end was originally sham and did not open at all. At this point, to the visitor's surprise, framed by the columns, Adam presented the Venetian window and panoramic prospect across the landscaped grounds towards London. The window contains a door, which allowed Lord Mansfield to invite his travel-weary guests straight out on to the terrace to enjoy the magnificent setting.

By the time they reached Kenwood such guests might have endured some discomfort, travelling the three miles (4.8km) uphill from central London by carriage. Standing beside this triple window they would have been struck by the villa's superb location, high on a ridge linking Highgate and Hampstead. Before the trees grew to their present height beyond the lakes, you could admire the London skyline. Guests would also have appreciated the illusion

of a great river rolling by, as if they were beside the Thames, complete with a sham bridge. This architectural feature masked the end of the lake, while drawing the eye towards the capital's most familiar landmark, the dome of St Paul's.

The plainer, more traditional late Palladian interior of the Ante Chamber, designed by Robert Adam's younger brother James in 1764, increases by contrast the impact of the Great Room. Another reason for the lack of lavish decoration is the room's dual role. Like the entrance hall, in this compact villa the Ante Chamber could serve various functions, depending on the time of day and type of visitor. Furnished with benches and opening on to Lord Mansfield's dressing room opposite the Great Room, it could have served as a smart waiting room for visitors here on business, particularly clients seeking an early-morning audience with the nation's leading lawyer.

As you enter the Great Room or Library, you can imagine the double doors opening before you as you step into the bustle of a grand reception.

The Ante Chamber, designed by James Adam in 1764

The Library or 'Great Room'

This vast saloon is considered by many to be Robert Adam's masterpiece, and as such one of the finest interiors of eighteenth-century Britain. The second part of Adam's *Works in Architecture*, published in 1774, is devoted to Kenwood. Here he explains that the 'Great Room', begun in 1767 and completed three years later, 'was intended both for a library and a room for receiving company. The circular recesses were therefore fitted up for the former purpose, and the square part, or body of the room, was made suitable to the latter'. The apse ends are not so much places for study as galleries for a bibliophile's collection, to be admired by his guests. The room would have been difficult to heat and, when alone, Lord

Mansfield would have withdrawn to his Dressing Room, which doubled as his study, taking any books he needed with him. The main attraction for guests, however, was not the early editions and fine bindings, nor the elaborate ceiling and fitted paintings by Zucchi, but the prospect south from the windows. There were no other views out, the north wall being mirrored to conceal the service buildings, kitchen gardens and public road that originally lay beyond.

Mansfield is known to have been a modest man but in this room pride of place above the chimneypiece is given to his portrait. The present overmantel is a copy, painted in 1994, of the original now at Scone Palace. Also in the room today, as in the eighteenth century, is a marble bust of Mansfield by Joseph Nollekens (1737–1823). Adam had originally proposed an historical subject for the overmantel, showing the administration of Roman justice. His patron's preference for a portrait of himself points to the fact that the room became something of a shrine to Mansfield. Newspaper articles and diaries of the late eighteenth century describe how admirers visiting the house in Mansfield's absence would be shown into this room by the housekeeper, where its busts and portraits would stand in for the great man himself.

The details of the decoration further reinforce this interpretation of the room as a celebration of the accomplishments of the self-made Lord Chief Justice. The gilded lions and stags' heads allude to the Mansfield coat of arms. The central ceiling painting, showing *Hercules between Glory and the Passions*, painted by Zucchi in 1769, is an allusion to wise judgement. The four lunettes represent *Justice embracing Peace*; *Commerce*; *Navigation*; and *Agriculture* in allusion to Mansfield's interests. The roundels show the four seasons while the four remaining panels contain symbolic figures of *Religion*, *Jurisprudence*, *Mathematics* and *Philosophy*.

Hercules appears again above the entrance door, as an infant strangling serpents. The walls of the apses are decorated with classical subjects on related themes: a copy of *The Aldobrandini Marriage: an Epithalamium* (a marriage song); *The Rape of Europa*; a *Bacchanal*; and *Minerva among the Arts*.

In scale and plan, with its columnar screened apses, the Great Room is inspired by the baths of ancient Rome. In his *Works* Adam describes in detail the shape of the ceiling, which 'is in the form and style of those of the ancients. It is an imitation of a flat arch, which is extremely beautiful, and much more perfect than that which is commonly called the coved ceiling [which] seems to be altogether of modern invention'. (An example of the traditional coved ceiling, embellished by the Adam brothers, can be found in the Ante Chamber.)

The vast pier-glasses between the windows and three curtain cornices are all that remained of the furniture designed by Adam for this room after the Kenwood auction of 1922. The mirrors were magnificent symbols of Mansfield's status, for such expanses of glass could not be made in England before 1780 and had to be imported from Venice and France. A visitor in 1776, Samuel Curwen, remarked that the room 'contains the largest mirrors I ever saw'. They took eight men three days to install.

Thomas Chippendale supplied the mirrors for the two recesses in 1769. From 1815 the recesses were lined with bookshelves and the present mirrors and gilded decoration are modern restorations

Now return to the Ante Chamber, turn right towards the north wing and pass through the double doors.

The Dining Room Lobby

You have now left the reception suite created by Robert Adam for the first Earl of Mansfield and entered the Dining Room wing, which today houses the finest paintings from the collection of Edward Cecil Guinness, first Earl of Iveagh. The lower light levels are intended to reduce glare from the windows so that visitors can enjoy the paintings to the full.

This is one of a pair of brick wings added between 1793 and 1796 by David Murray, second Earl of Mansfield (see page 30). Together they formed an extension to Adam's reception suite, providing a dining room on this side and a drawing room or Music Room across the hall, with bedrooms above. As a former ambassador to Vienna and Paris the second Earl must have found the economical use of space in his uncle's villa socially limiting, particularly the use of the entrance hall as a formal dining room.

Two doors in the east wall (to your right) lead to the Service Wing, which the second Earl also built to support his more lavish lifestyle. As food would have been brought into this lobby

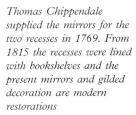

In the central ceiling painting by Zucchi, Hercules turns from the tempting pleasures of the flesh to take up his club and shield and follow the rocky path to eternal fame, represented by a distant temple

ABOVE RIGHT *Hercules appears again above the doorway into the room, as an infant strangling serpents, painted by Zucchi in 1769*

before being served in the Dining Room, the floor was protected by a 'floorcloth', the forerunner of linoleum, consisting of layers of oil paint on canvas. The present floorcloth was created in 2000 based on eighteenth-century designs.

The two mirrors are rare examples of Kenwood's historic furniture before Adam's engagement here. They were probably supplied by King George III's cabinet-maker William France to hang in the Upper Hall when it formed the principal apartment. Sold in 1922, they were brought back to Kenwood in 1994.

A Coast Scene with Fishermen Hauling a Boat Ashore was painted by JMW Turner (1775 - 1851) when he was about twenty-eight years old, and the most successful, controversial and challenging artist of his generation

THE REDECORATION OF THE NORTH WINGS

Lord Iveagh died before he could redecorate and furnish Kenwood and hang his collection here. From 1928, when the house opened to the public, to the end of the

twentieth century, the Dining Room and its ante chamber lacked historic decoration, curtains and carpets. Polished wooden flooring reflected glare from the tall windows, white shutters, doors and dado, making it difficult to see the paintings. To mark the year 2000 these rooms and the corresponding pair in the other north wing were the subject of the most extensive interior refurbishment in the history of the house as a museum. Crucial to the redecoration project was the reduction in light levels, in order that the paintings could be seen as the brightest points of interest in each room.

English Heritage consulted a wide variety of sources in devising a suitable decorative scheme for the rooms. Full-scale restoration was ruled out: the Dining Room curtains and furniture (with the exception of the two original sideboards) were lost, and none of the historical schemes was felt to be conducive to the appreciation of the

seventeenth-century Dutch and Flemish masterpieces of the Iveagh Bequest. The Dining Room had never served as a picture gallery, the Earls of Mansfield hanging at most nine family portraits in this room.

Nevertheless historical evidence for these rooms contributed to the new scheme. Further inspiration was derived from Lord Iveagh's Dublin home, Farmleigh, and from other art museums founded by collectors in the same inter-war period, notably The Frick Collection in New York. Two Irish houses near Dublin were also consulted: Russborough, which houses the Beit Collection; and Newbridge where the dining room curtains and their poles have remained, exceptionally, *in situ* since 1828.

The scheme that was eventually adopted is a creative amalgam of all these sources, the paintings themselves being the ultimate point of reference.

The Dining Room

Most of the paintings in the Iveagh Bequest can be grouped into two artistic schools: seventeenth-century Dutch and Flemish masters, and British portrait painters of the eighteenth and early nineteenth centuries. The former school can be found in the Dining Room (with some relevant British paintings) and some of the finest of the latter in the Music Room.

Two supreme masterpieces of international significance hang in the Dining Room: Rembrandt's celebrated self-portrait, painted around 1665, and Vermeer's *Guitar Player* painted around 1672. Rembrandt's self-portrait is paired with a portrait of an unknown lady by his pupil, Ferdinand Bol (1616–80). Above them hang paintings by Sir Joshua Reynolds (1723–92) in Rembrandt's manner, to provide visitors with an opportunity to compare the artists. Such juxtapositions can be found in country houses but are unusual in museums and public galleries where paintings are generally arranged by nationality and period. As a collection formed by one man, rather than by a family or generations of curators, the Iveagh Bequest also provides an opportunity to consider the taste of Lord Iveagh and the subjects that most appealed to this late Victorian businessman and philanthropist.

Now return to the Venetian window in the Ante Chamber and turn right into Lord Mansfield's Dressing Room.

The South Front Rooms

Along the south front of Kenwood, behind the reception rooms and bordering the terrace, is a suite of rooms comprising the former family apartments. The present sequence of aligned doorways dates only from 1925–28 when Kenwood was converted for use as an art gallery. In the eighteenth century there were four rooms: Lord and Lady Mansfield's dressing rooms (directly below their bedrooms upstairs), and between them a parlour, where they would have breakfasted and dined with their nieces, and a drawing room. The central wall dividing the parlour from the drawing room was removed by the architect William Atkinson (*c.*1773–1839) for the third Earl of Mansfield (1777–1840) in 1815. Beyond lies the Orangery, a free-standing greenhouse which Adam linked on to the main house via an ante chamber, complete with a Venetian window. Adam designed the Library to balance symmetrically with the Orangery and so gave the villa an elegant long façade to face the public road, Millfield Lane, which ran straight

The Breakfast Room in 1913 when it served as the study of Grand Duke Michael Michaelovich, the exiled grandson of Tsar Nicholas I (see page 32)

CENTRE Marble bust of Lady Mansfield carved around 1745 by Louis François Roubiliac (1705–62)

'Pier-glass in the Parlour' designed by Adam and supplied by George Burns in 1772, as illustrated in an engraving in the Kenwood section of Adam's Works in Architecture

up to Hampstead Lane at that time. Today these former family apartments are presented primarily as galleries of paintings, as they were throughout most of the twentieth century. There are no longer any paintings in the Orangery, however, as it was a greenhouse and the unstable climate makes it unsuitable for works of art.

Lord Mansfield's Dressing Room

The earliest account of this room appears in an article published in the *Morning Herald* on 21 September 1781. Entitled 'A Peep into Lord Mansfield's Villa Caen Wood', it describes the house almost as if it were a celebrity's home that one might wish to visit. Lord Mansfield's Dressing Room was clearly the great judge's inner sanctum where he would despatch daily business, receive his steward and give instructions for the estate, while being dressed by his manservant. It was also his study where he kept some of his prized possessions:

> The room his Lordship usually reads in, is thus well hung; for besides the two before mentioned portraits of Betterton and Garrick, there are some good drawings of Raffaelle, and that modern Salvator Rosa, 'the rapid Mortimer.' The book upon his Lordship's table, and which apparently he had been lately perusing, was 'Weskett upon Commerce'.

The room also contained a marble bust of Homer (now at Scone Palace) bequeathed to Mansfield by his mentor, the poet Alexander Pope (see page 23), who believed it to be by the Italian sculptor Bernini.

The Breakfast Room

This room was created in 1815 by combining the drawing room (adjacent to Lord Mansfield's Study) with the parlour. Previously the parlour would have served as the family dining room and, like the drawing room, could have been reached through doors that opened direct from the entrance hall. When the wall was removed a new cornice united the two rooms and bookcases were installed to provide a large study for the third Earl of Mansfield.

An inventory of 1831 calls this the 'Breakfast Room'; it also records the presence of fine

furniture, including four large mirrors on the window wall, three 'superb' pier-tables each 'inlaid and ornamented with brass on 8 legs', fourteen cane-seated chairs and four 'flower stands painted green'.

Lady Mansfield's Dressing Room

In Adam's unpublished plan of Kenwood this room is divided into two, with a 'China Closet' at the northern end and the two doorways near the window. The room today is the result of alterations made around 1926–27. Here Lady Mansfield would have undertaken the domestic administration of Kenwood; her housekeeper's room is immediately adjacent. Like her half-niece Lady Burlington at Chiswick House, she kept a small room for her collection of porcelain. The dressing room must have served also as her study, for in 1770 a joiner was paid to fit bookcase doors in the room. No evidence of its decoration has been found but in 1776 Horace Walpole wrote to the Revd William Mason describing 'a Theban harp, as beautifully and gracefully designed as if Mr Adam had drawn it from Lady Mansfield's dressing room, with a sphinx, masks, a patera, and a running foliage of leaves'.

The Housekeeper's Room

Like the Ante Chamber to the Library, this room is dominated by a Venetian or 'Palladian' window, only here it serves to balance the external symmetry of the façade rather than to provide guests with a picturesque view. If such a window seems an extravagance for a housekeeper's room it may be because Lady Mansfield found it too draughty for her own use. Pope praised Lord Burlington, the champion of Palladian architecture, for introducing such Italian architectural features in his new villa, Chiswick House, but mocked his followers for their lack of regard for the British climate:

> … Your noble Rules
> Fill half the Land with *Imitating Fools* …
> Proud to catch cold at a *Venetian door.*
> (*Epistle to Lord Burlington*, 1731)

In the first Earl of Mansfield's day the service wing lay directly north of this room, thereby connecting the housekeeper to the kitchens. The Orangery was not accessible from the house, but from a garden door at the opposite end.

The Orangery

Adam's plan of Kenwood, published in 1774, identifies this room as the 'Green House'. In 1780 an article on Kenwood in *The Ambulator* calls the potential visitor's attention to its contents: 'The green house also is superb, and contains a very large collection of curious and exotic plants, trees, &c'. No plant list has yet been found but we may imagine the colourful fragrant room filled with tubs of orange trees, peach trees and myrtle (brought in from the terrace in winter), together with geraniums, sweet marjorams and lavender. The flagstone floor lay three inches lower than the rest of the house, for this was originally a free-standing building, constructed before Adam built the Library wing to balance it. The exotic produce would have been warmed by air from the kitchens and bake house which adjoined the north wall in the eighteenth century. The co-location of service wing and greenhouse had other benefits, as Humphry Repton recalled in 1803: 'At Caenwood, at Thoresby, and some other large houses of the last century, green-houses were added to conceal offices behind them'. With the addition of the Music Room wing by the second Earl from 1793 the Orangery was linked to the house via large glazed doors.

From the Orangery, complete your tour of the ground floor by passing through the glass doors into the second wing added by the second Earl of Mansfield between 1793 and 1796.

The prospect south from the Orangery looking across the terrace towards the sham bridge

The Green Room

This wing of the house, comprising a drawing
room and its ante chamber, was added by the
architect George Saunders (*c*.1762–1839) for the
second Earl of Mansfield as part of the general
enlargement of Kenwood undertaken by the
Earl on inheriting the house from his uncle in
1793; the building works were completed by
1796. It links via the entrance hall to his other
addition, the Dining Room wing, and together
they provided a substantial extension to the
reception suite created by Robert Adam from
1764 to 1773.

All the windows in this wing face west, to
benefit from the afternoon and evening sunlight.
The second Earl removed the kitchens, bake
house and servants' quarters from this side of
the house after creating a new Service Wing to
the east. In their place he and his heir, the third

Earl, laid out a colourful flower garden with
crescent-shaped beds. Looking out at the west
lawn today we can only imagine such a scene,
for the last vestiges of a formal garden were
swept away in 1966. The prospect was crowned
by the dairy, an ornamental farm building to
which guests would stroll to take tea and admire
the views over the estate (see page 30). The
dairy still survives but in the twentieth century
the view of it from this room became obscured
by trees. The windows of this wing were
extended down to their present length in 1850
when the veranda was constructed.

Throughout the twentieth century these two
rooms were simply painted off-white from floor
to ceiling, with modern flooring, no carpeting
and minimal curtains at the Music Room
windows. The millennium year re-presentation
project sought to reduce glare caused by a
surfeit of daylight and to make the paintings the
lightest, and thus focal, points in each room.

The position of the rooms, between a
greenhouse and a floral garden, provided
inspiration for their redecoration and the re-
hanging of Lord Iveagh's paintings. Whereas the
Dining Room wing is dominated by
Rembrandt's sublime self-portrait, around which
are grouped seventeenth-century Dutch and
Flemish masterpieces and works by their British
admirers, the Music Room wing is home to
Gainsborough's *Countess Howe*, which forms the
finale to two rooms of portraits of society
beauties, children and French Rococo fantasies.
Together these paintings help to recreate the
atmosphere of a lady's drawing room opening
on to gardens.

In the Green Room, the choice of colours
and carpet is indebted to analysis of the
surviving paint layers, to the watercolour view
of 1824 (above left), to manufacturers' archives
and to the paintings themselves.

The Music Room

This is, quite simply, one of the great rooms of
British art. Gainsborough's *Countess Howe* holds
her court among society beauties and *demi-
mondaines* painted by Reynolds, Romney
(1734–1802), Hoppner (1758–1810) and
Gainsborough himself. In assembling this
personal harem – portraits of men by British

artists are almost absent from the Iveagh Bequest – Lord Iveagh was buying some of the most fashionable names on the art market.

Many of the subjects would have known one another: for example, Countess Howe has been hung paired (for the first time) with her niece Mrs Musters, painted by Reynolds. More familiar names today are those of the actress Mrs Jordan (by Hoppner), the courtesan Kitty Fisher (by Reynolds) and Emma Hart (by Romney).

Lady Hamilton at the Spinning Wheel *by George Romney, painted between 1782 and 1786 when Emma Hart was the mistress of Charles Greville. She left him for his uncle, Sir William Hamilton, in 1786, and later became the mistress of Lord Nelson (detail)*

Above the door hangs a scene of musical *putti* (cherubs) painted by Julius Caesar Ibbetson (1759–1817) who worked at Kenwood from 1794 to 1797 (see page 31). This is a fragment of a larger scheme of decorative borders painted by Ibbetson for this room, which was dismantled in 1927 to provide space for Lord Iveagh's paintings.

The chamber organ on the end wall, made by John England and Son around 1790, is a replacement, purchased by English Heritage, for a similar one by Robert and William Gray that was supplied in 1796 for this position. Still in working order, it is used for occasional recitals and helps to evoke some idea of how guests would have enjoyed this room in the evenings. They would have withdrawn here from the Dining Room (by way of the hall) for some musical entertainment, possibly ending their reception in the Green Room, which was

described in 1816 as the 'Supper Room'. A door between the column screen and the Orangery leads to a staircase which originally led to bedrooms overhead.

Return now to the entrance hall via the bookshop.

The Upper Hall

The Upper Hall contains further paintings. From the entrance hall take the door to the left of the chimneypiece and ascend the staircase. Half-way up the stairs a room to the left now contains two collections of portrait miniatures: the Draper Gift and the collection formed by Bernard Falk, the latter on generous long-term loan from his family. The display also includes a selection from the Lady Maufe Collection of Georgian Shoebuckles and costume jewellery presented to Kenwood by Anne Hull Grundy.

The Upper Hall and adjoining rooms are regularly used for temporary exhibitions, and their permanent decoration is therefore kept to a minimum. Before Adam added the Great Room downstairs, the Upper Hall would have served as the principal apartment for receiving company in the house; it commanded a fine view north across Hampstead Lane before the second Earl diverted the road and planted up Prospect Hill as a screen. After the Library was built it was used by the first Earl, his wife and nieces as a morning room, along with the three bedrooms. A feature of great interest is the chimneypiece designed by Robert Adam in the *chinoiserie* taste. The room was also hung with Chinese wallpaper, one fragment of which survives. The panelled doors date from the early eighteenth century and were retained by Adam. By 1816 the room was being used for billiards.

Mrs Elizabeth Farren *by Andrew Plimer (1763–1837) painted around 1785. Elizabeth Farren was a celebrated actress and beauty, and long-time mistress of the twelfth Earl of Derby whom she eventually married in 1797*

OPPOSITE Mary, Countess Howe *by Thomas Gainsborough (1727–88). This portrait of the wife of the naval hero Earl Howe was painted around 1763–4 soon after the artist moved to Bath. The elegance and aristocratic demeanour which Gainsborough bestows on his subject reflect his study of seventeenth-century portraits by Van Dyck in neighbouring country houses such as Wilton and Corsham Court*

The chimneypiece, designed by Adam and carved by Sefferin Nelson in 1773, incorporates Chinese painted marble tiles

THE
⮚ GARDENS AND ESTATE ⮘

In the first Earl of Mansfield's time the view from the terrace at Kenwood appeared to be broad and expansive but the gardens of the 90-acre (37ha) landscape were actually fairly constrained between two enclosing walls running from north to south. A public footpath and Fitzroy Farm lay within 100 yards (91m) of the east side of the house. Lord Bute's formal planting remained in an 8-acre (3ha) garden between the house and the ponds, which appears in Wootton's painting of the view from the terrace (below). Lord Mansfield merged the four fish ponds to create the 'Thousand Pound Pond' (so called from its cost) terminated by the sham bridge to give the illusion of a river flowing by.

By the time the second Earl of Mansfield commissioned Humphry Repton to produce a 'Red Book' of proposals in 1793 the estate extended over 232 acres (94ha) and reached south beyond Highgate Ponds and Parliament Hill to Gospel Oak, where Mansfield Road still marks the boundary. To the north, a further 700 acres (284ha) had been leased by the first Earl from the Bishop of London to serve as farmland, reaching as far as Hornsey and the present North Circular Road. However, the pleasure gardens around the house must have appeared old-fashioned. The two wings which

Kenwood, the south front from the pond, *drawn by Mary Delany in 1756, the year after William Murray purchased Kenwood (detail)*

A View from Caenwood House over London *painted by John Wootton in 1755*

OPPOSITE *The gardens today, seen from the lake*

the second Earl added to the entrance front of Kenwood provided family accommodation but also opened up new views of the gardens from the house; visitors were no longer led just to the terrace and the fine southern prospect towards the London skyline but could look west across a new flower garden and north to woodlands, following the diversion of Hampstead Lane. The clutter of farmyard and service buildings to the north-east of the house was cleared away and the present Service Wing, stables, gate lodges and dairy were created. An octagonal farmhouse, designed by the agriculturist William Marshall, became the focus of a new 200-acre (81ha) model farm.

The sham bridge escaped Repton's recommendation that it be demolished. (He

'Before' (right) and 'after' (below): Repton's proposal for the south front in 1793 included a viaduct over a grand approach drive from Millfield Lane

wrote: 'It is a deception so frequently liable to be detected, I think it is an object beneath the dignity of Kenwood.') Today, the Kenwood estate is an exceptional survivor in greater London, with most of its outbuildings intact. Unfortunately, the designed landscape suffered in the second half of the twentieth century from cuts in maintenance expenditure encouraged by the romantic misapprehension that the estate should be left to run wild, as part of the public open space known as Hampstead Heath. In fact, of the 802 acres (325ha) now known as the Heath, only 220 acres (89ha) were the common lands of the Manor of Hampstead. At its most extensive Kenwood's parkland and farmland extended over 1,500 acres (608ha).

Since 1990 English Heritage has undertaken extensive repairs to preserve the estate's character and importance as an historic designed parkland. As J C Loudon wrote in his *Suburban Gardener* (1838): 'This is, beyond all question, the finest country residence in the suburbs of London …. It is, indeed, difficult to imagine a more retired or more romantic spot, and yet of such extent, so near a great metropolis.'

The Service Wing

The Service Wing was built by George Saunders for the second Earl of Mansfield between 1793 and 1796, and completed by Saunders in 1797 for the third Earl. The previous service wing stood behind the Orangery. Demolition allowed space for a new Music Room, and opened up the view west from the room towards the dairy and the afternoon sun.

The new Service Wing was built of rare purple-brown London stocks, in deliberate contrast to the white bricks used by Saunders for the additions to the main house. It was clearly intended to be as inconspicuous as possible, and the embankment of the terrace helped both to conceal the building from the pleasure garden, and to block the servants' view of their masters at leisure.

Including the adjacent cellars beneath the Adam Library and north wing, the Service Wing contains a warren of over sixty rooms. These include beer and wine cellars, servants' quarters, a wash house, pantry and all other

rooms necessary to the daily running of a gentleman's family seat, contrasting with the more modest requirements of the smaller villa frequented by the first Earl. The earliest dated plan of the wing, from 1815, includes thirteen bedrooms for staff, some large enough for several servants.

The largest room is the vast kitchen, which originally rose the full height of the Service Wing. It is entered through the loggia of columns opposite the eighteenth-century Cold Bath. The kitchen is open occasionally for special events and may be booked for private functions; the restaurant occupies the old laundry and brew house alongside. These are the only service rooms open to the public at present. The octagonal plan of the kitchen was suggested to Saunders by Humphry Repton, who had in mind the medieval Abbot's Kitchen at Glastonbury.

To reach the second Earl's dining table from this kitchen, food had to travel along the corridor behind the open colonnade and into the basement of the Dining Room wing. Here a stone staircase leads up to the Dining Room lobby. Communication over such distances was only possible from the end of the eighteenth century, when the bell-pull was developed into an elaborate system employing wires and cranks.

The trellis arbour leading from the flower garden on to the terrace, as illustrated in J C Loudon's The Surburban Gardener, *1838*

The Old Kitchen in the Service Wing, with its Victorian grate, spit, baking oven and warming cupboards (open for special events and private functions)

THE CREATORS OF
～ KENWOOD ～

Marble bust of the first Earl of Mansfield carved by Joseph Nollekens in 1779, inscribed with Mansfield's motto Uni Æquus Virtuti *(Faithful Unto Virtue Alone)*

Early Owners

The original house was probably built by John Bill, the King's Printer, shortly after he purchased the estate in 1616. From 1694 to 1704 Kenwood belonged to William Bridges, Surveyor General of the Ordnance at the Tower of London, to whom may be attributed the brick double-pile house that still survives inside Adam's alterations. The earliest known images, from 1755 and 1756 (see below and page 19), show a house with steeply pitched roof and dormer windows, covered with stucco.

From 1712 Kenwood belonged to a succession of Scots, beginning with John Campbell, second Duke of Argyll, who in 1715 conveyed it jointly to his brother, the Earl of Ilay, and his brother-in-law, James Stuart, second Earl of Bute. In 1720 they sold it to an upholsterer of Covent Garden who mortgaged it

back to them before losing a fortune he had made from investing in the South Sea Bubble. Kenwood was then rented from 1725 by George Middleton, a partner in what later became Coutts Bank, until his death in 1747.

In 1746 the Earl of Ilay conveyed his share of Kenwood to his nephew, John Stuart, third Earl of Bute, who had already inherited his father's half share. In 1750 Bute became Lord of the Bedchamber to Frederick, Prince of Wales but found time to repair, redecorate and refurbish Kenwood, plant specimen trees and father five children. Bute is best known today as one of this country's most unpopular prime ministers, a position he held from 1762 to 1763. In 1751 he wrote to the Dutch scholar Gronovius describing 'a garden of 8 acres betwixt me and the wood, I am filling with every exotick our climate will protect'. In 1754 Bute sold Kenwood to a rising lawyer and fellow Scot, William Murray.

The earliest known view of Kenwood, in the background of Heath House, Hampstead *by T Ramsey, 1755 (detail)*

William Murray, First Earl of Mansfield

William Murray was the fourth son of the fifth Viscount Stormont, the latter being a noted Jacobite who was imprisoned in 1715 for supporting the 'Old Pretender' to the British throne, James Stuart. Murray left the family seat, Scone Palace, Perthshire, when he was thirteen, never to return. Following study at Westminster School, Christ Church, Oxford and Lincoln's Inn he entered the House of Commons in 1742 and was immediately appointed Solicitor General, at the age of thirty-seven. His portrait by Van Loo (right) was probably commissioned to mark the occasion. As a promising young lawyer Murray enjoyed the company of the poet Alexander Pope and the literary circle that frequented Pope's villa at Twickenham.

In 1754 Murray was appointed Attorney General and in the same year he purchased Kenwood; two years later he was appointed Chief Justice of the Court of King's Bench and raised to the peerage as the first Earl of Mansfield. His many achievements as a judge include reforming mercantile law, reducing religious discrimination and improving court procedure, but he is best known today for a ruling that made slavery illegal in England (see page 29). A renowned orator, 'silver-tongued Murray' was the ablest defender of the Government in Parliament, particularly against his life-long foe William Pitt the Elder, Earl of Chatham.

The great judge achieved celebrity status in his day, both among young lawyers who would admire their hero from the public galleries when he was in court, and among politicians for his wit in parliamentary debate. Souvenir portraits of him were reproduced, and the political theorist Jeremy Bentham, when a student of laws, was said to have 'kept, as a great treasure, a picture of him, and frequently went to Caen Wood, as a lover to the shrine of his mistress, in the hope that chance might throw him his way'.

Although the most fashionable villas in the eighteenth century were situated beside the Thames at Richmond and Twickenham, Kenwood's location suited Murray. Highgate had clean air and had been favoured by lawyers from at least the seventeenth century as it was

William Murray, later first Earl of Mansfield, *after Jan Baptiste Van Loo (1684–1745), painted around 1742*

CENTRE *Detail of John Wootton's view from the terrace at Kenwood, 1755 (see page 19) showing Lord Mansfield, his guest W Hoskins and Wootton himself, sketching the view*

OPPOSITE View of the South Front of the Villa at Kenwood, *from Robert Adam's* Works

Lady Elizabeth and Lady Henrietta Finch, *painted by Charles Jervas around 1732. The future wife of the first Earl of Mansfield is on the left, making a crown of myrtle as if to crown a suitor*

conveniently situated for reaching both the Inns of Court in the City of London and Westminster Hall (which housed the Law Courts until 1882).

Murray had married Lady Elizabeth Finch (1704–84), daughter of the second Earl of Nottingham and the seventh Earl of Winchelsea, in 1738 when she was thirty-four. Her choice of the young lawyer, who was several months her junior, was regarded by some as a marriage beneath her aristocratic station, prompted by her advancing years. The writer Lady Mary Wortley Montagu remarked: 'People are divided in their opinions, as they commonly are, on the prudence of her choice. I am among those who think *tout bien compté*, she has happily disposed of her person.' The couple had no children of their own, but raised four of their nieces at Kenwood (see page 28).

Lady Elizabeth Finch.

Robert Adam at Kenwood

The Earl of Bute was probably responsible for introducing Murray to Robert Adam in or before 1764. Adam was a rising star among architects: having returned from study in Italy in 1758 he was appointed Architect of the King's Works (jointly with William Chambers) in 1761 and in 1764 he published the results of his archaeological research in Dalmatia, *Ruins of the Palace of the Emperor Diocletian at Spalatro*. Murray had by this time been raised to the peerage and needed a grand reception room, a fashionable dining room and a third storey to provide additional bedrooms, for his villa was much in demand for meetings with fellow judges, bishops and leading politicians from the Prime Minister down. Lord Mansfield was regarded by many as a 'closet' Prime Minister, giving secret advice to the sovereign, George III.

Adam's brief from his patron is not recorded, but in the lavish folio of engravings he published in 1774 to commemorate the commission (part of his *Works in Architecture*) he praises 'Lord Mansfield, the friend of every elegant art', who 'gave full scope to my ideas'. Evidently architect and patron agreed on their aims: to remodel the villa, inside and out, from the portico down to the doorknobs, in the fashionable neoclassical style; and to give it a grandeur befitting the rising status of its owner and his eminent guests.

Adam accordingly created the 'Library' wing, balancing it with the earlier Orangery (which he attached to the villa) and then united the whole of the exterior with stucco ornament. The third storey was added and an imposing portico defined the main entrance on the north front, then facing Hampstead Lane.

Adam was greatly inspired by the view from Kenwood, and his remodelling of the villa was strongly influenced by his desire to make the most of this advantage. (The view, across the sham bridge and towards St Paul's Cathedral, can be seen in the background of the painting of Mansfield's nieces reproduced on page 28.)

The decoration of the south front, first completed in 1773, shows the refined linear exterior ornament which Adam pioneered at Kenwood. Such façades were 'no better than models for the Twelfth-Night-Decoration of a Pastry Cook', according to a pamphlet published in 1779

Detail of the column supporting the portico over the entrance, designed by Robert Adam in 1768

RIGHT *The balustrade to Adam's 'Great Stairs' doubles as a decorative screen*

In his publication on Kenwood Adam set the scene:

> Over the vale, through which the water flows, there is a noble view let into the house and terrace, of the city of London, Greenwich Hospital, the River Thames, the ships passing up and down, with an extensive prospect, but clear and distinct, on both sides of the river. To the north-east, and west of the house and terrace the mountainous villages of Highgate and Hampstead form delightful objects. The whole scene is amazingly gay, magnificent, beautiful and picturesque ....

Adam's use of the term 'picturesque' reveals one of his principles as an architect. The word was more often used to describe a landscape garden that had been remodelled to resemble paintings by Claude or Poussin, but Adam, who himself sketched landscape, explained in the preface to his *Works in Architecture* how the picturesque could also influence buildings:

> *Movement* is meant to express, the rise and fall, the advance and recess, with other diversity of form, in the different parts of a building, so as to add greatly to the picturesque of the composition.

This concept is well exemplified in the contrasting rooms of the reception suite.

Adam took a great pride in his work at Kenwood, doubtless seeing his eminent patron

and the prominent location of his London villa as an ideal opportunity to advertise his genius for converting older houses into the most fashionable residences. By contrast, many of the great houses with which we identify Adam today (such as Harewood, Kedleston, Croome Court, Osterley, Newby Hall, Saltram and Bowood) are not mentioned in the *Works*.

KENWOOD ESCAPES THE GORDON RIOTS

Detail of Lord Mansfield *by David Martin, 1775*

Kenwood was nearly burnt to the ground on 6 June 1780 during the Gordon Riots. As Lord Chief Justice, Mansfield sought to protect the rights of Protestant Dissenters and Roman Catholics but was suspected of being a Jacobite, Papist and even a Jesuit. In 1778 the Catholic Relief Bill was introduced to repeal an act from the reign of William III that had made it difficult for a Roman Catholic to own land by inheritance or purchase, to serve as a schoolmaster, or for a priest to say Mass. Opposition to the Bill in the House of Commons was led by Lord George Gordon, president of the 'General Protestant Association'. On 2 June 1780 a crowd estimated to be 60,000 strong took possession of the streets surrounding the Houses of Parliament, and over the following week houses and shops were looted and burned, including Lord Mansfield's house in Bloomsbury Square. After throwing his furniture, library and collection of classical and medieval manuscripts from the windows to fuel a bonfire, the mob armed themselves with the house's iron railings. Brandishing a noose and ringing Mansfield's dinner bell to rally more support, they marched north to Kenwood. Fortunately Mansfield's steward at Kenwood and the landlord of the Spaniard's Inn on Hampstead Lane were prepared and provided free ale at the roadside. Meanwhile Mansfield's nephew Lord Stormont, a Secretary of State, sent 'a detachment of light horse' to intercept them. Following the destruction of his town house Mansfield spent most of his time at Kenwood.

According to the *Hampstead and Highgate Express*, reporting in 1928:

> A curiosity of the house is a room in the basement still known as the guard room. The military guard that it once accommodated was furnished by the first Lord Mansfield for his protection after the Gordon Riots, and the old muskets were there until lately.

Engraving after The Gordon Riots *by John Seymour Lucas*

Dido Belle, Lord Mansfield's black great-niece, is first recorded at Kenwood in this detail of A View from Caenwood House over London *(see page 19)*

PRIVATE COLLECTION

Mansfield's Great-Niece, Dido Belle

The first Earl of Mansfield had no children but he and Lady Mansfield raised two generations of nieces at Kenwood: Anne and Marjory Murray (sisters of his nephew and heir, David seventh Viscount Stormont); and Lord Stormont's eldest daughter, Elizabeth, whose mother had died in 1766. Lord Stormont served abroad as ambassador to Vienna and Paris. Elizabeth had as her companion her black cousin, Dido Elizabeth Belle. Dido's father was Mansfield's other nephew, Sir John Lindsay, a Rear Admiral in the Royal Navy; her mother was a slave, whom Sir John had encountered in a captured Spanish ship. He brought her to England where Dido was born but her mother's fate is unknown. Dido is recorded as a toddler on the terrace at Kenwood (left) and as a beautiful teenager in the double portrait with Elizabeth (below; now in the Mansfield collection at Scone Palace), where she wears a plumed turban and carries exotic fruit. Dido clearly held an ambiguous status, as neither a servant nor a fully fledged member of the family. She superintended the dairy and probably left Kenwood shortly after Lord Mansfield's death in 1793, when she married a Mr Davinier. In his will, Mansfield left her an annual income of £100 for life and took the precaution of confirming her freedom from slavery.

Elizabeth Murray sits on a garden bench on the terrace at Kenwood and looks up from her studies as her cousin, Dido Belle, strolls past carrying grapes, peaches and pears from the Orangery and garden. Both women were great-nieces of the first Earl of Mansfield. The painting is unattributed but dates from around 1770. It also records Kenwood's fine prospect towards the City of London

THE EARL OF MANSFIELD, SCONE PALACE

MANSFIELD AND THE STATUS OF SLAVES IN ENGLAND

The most celebrated judgement of Britain's greatest lawyer was over a runaway slave. James Sommersett came to England from Virginia in 1769 with his master but escaped, only to be recaptured and put on a ship to Jamaica to be sold. Opponents of the slave trade campaigned for his release and in 1772 sought to make a test case before the Court of King's Bench. They questioned whether a slave could be deemed another man's property, and thus held against his will, within the jurisdiction of English law. Mansfield delayed making a decision, anticipating serious repercussions if he were to rule in favour of Sommersett. Finally, however, he announced his decision, which was described at the time as 'guarded, cautious, and concise':

> The state of slavery … is so odious, that nothing can be suffered to support it, but positive law. Whatever inconvenience, therefore, may follow from this decision I cannot say this case is allowed or approved by the law of England; and, therefore, the black must be discharged.

Wealthier black people celebrated at a 'Black Assembly' in Westminster, where 200 guests drank to Mansfield's health before ending the evening with a ball.

Mansfield's decision made it illegal to ship a person abroad to sell into slavery. Despite this, black people continued to be hunted and kidnapped in London, Liverpool

Anti-slavery pendant bearing the words 'Am I not a man and a brother?', designed by Josiah Wedgwood around 1787

and Bristol. Nor did his ruling abolish slavery itself in the British Empire.

Mansfield's special expertise in commercial law, particularly marine insurance, helped him with a second decision involving slavery. In 1781 an epidemic broke out on the slave ship *Zong*, containing 470 Africans. Believing he could claim insurance for slaves lost at sea, but not for those who died on board, the master of the ship chose 133 slaves and had them thrown over the side. The insurance underwriters disputed the claim made by the ship's owners but the trial found in the latter's favour. When the underwriters applied to the Court of King's Bench in 1782 Mansfield declared 'there should be a new trial'.

The position of black people remained vulnerable. In making his will the same year Mansfield took care to confirm the freedom of his great-niece Dido Belle. In 1787 the Society for the Abolition of the Slave Trade was founded, under the leadership in Parliament of William Wilberforce. In 1807 Parliament prohibited British subjects from taking part in the slave trade but it was not until 1833 that slavery itself was abolished in Britain and its empire.

The Second Earl and Repton

Lord Mansfield died in 1793, aged eighty-seven. His successor David, second Earl of Mansfield, aged sixty-six, was full of plans to turn Kenwood into his main family residence, in preference to Scone Palace. A former ambassador to Vienna and Paris, the second Earl was a connoisseur of art and, unlike his uncle, had formed a collection of paintings and French furniture, for which he would have found little room at Kenwood. On coming into his inheritance he commissioned the landscape architect Humphry Repton to produce a 'Red Book' of watercolour design proposals for the estate (rediscovered at Scone Palace in 1996).

Repton's recommendations also included the first Earl's unrealised ambitions. Hampstead Lane was diverted behind Prospect Hill to give the house a secluded setting at the end of serpentine drives. New estate buildings were constructed and the old ones swept away (see page 19).

Miniature of the second Earl of Mansfield, after a portrait by Pompeo Batoni, painted in Rome in 1768 when Murray was seventh Viscount Stormont

Repton's proposal for the north front included the creation of serpentine drives, the removal of service buildings and the addition of wings to the north façade

Repton's characteristic 'before and after' watercolours also included proposals for adding two wings to the north front. The new wings were to provide additional reception rooms and bedrooms above, without disturbing 'the grand façade to the south'. When the scheme was finally executed they were built using white bricks, Suffolk stocks, instead of continuing the stucco finish on the rest of the house, as proposed by Repton.

One reason for this change was the second Earl's wish that the new wings did not conflict with Adam's design. As the Earl noted on 6 August 1793, the day before he signed off the designs: 'It must be self-evident that these projecting wings were not built at the same time with the Body of the House …. The wings should be so built as to appear chaste simple Buildings in themselves.' The other reason, recalled by Repton, was the first Earl's bad experience of 'Liardet', a patent oil cement used by Adam which failed to adhere to the south front. As Repton recorded: 'The great Lord Mansfield often declared that had the front of Kenwood been originally covered in Parian marble, he should have found it less expensive than stucco.'

Robert Adam had died in 1792 and although the second Earl employed James Adam to alter his town house in Portland Place he engaged a relatively obscure architect, Robert Nasmith, to design the additions to Kenwood.

Louisa, Viscountess Stormont, drawn by Ozias Humphry in 1780

Nasmith in turn died on 30 August 1793 and was succeeded by the surveyor at Kenwood, George Saunders. Saunders also added the present Service Wing, stables, octagonal farmyard and dairy.

The interiors of the wings may have been inspired by some of the most fashionable work in London at the time, that of the architect Henry Holland at Carlton House, Pall Mall (demolished in 1827) for George, Prince of Wales (the future King George IV). There are some obvious parallels between the two, such as the circular balustrade balcony and skylight in the Dining Room Lobby, which recall the Octagon vestibule at Carlton House.

Louisa Cathcart, Countess of Mansfield

Louisa Cathcart (1758–1843), wife of the second Earl, had first visited Kenwood in January 1776 as the seventeen-year-old daughter of the widowed Lord Cathcart. Her two older sisters had recently married, and she had been chosen to be the second wife of David, Viscount Stormont, Lord Mansfield's nephew and heir. Stormont, then nearly fifty, had been widowed for some years, and as British ambassador in Paris was not at Kenwood that evening.

He returned to London in April, and the wedding took place at Kenwood on 5 May 1776. During her honeymoon, she wrote to her sister: 'You cannot imagine how happy and how much at home I am here …. This place is delightful, I never saw anything I liked more'.

As soon as Louisa and her husband, the new Earl and Countess, took over Kenwood in 1793 they began improving and expanding the house and estate. Louisa personally supervised the new buildings. Her influence is most clearly found on the west side of the house, in the Music Room overlooking the flower garden, and in the new dairy. The latter, in a picturesque rustic style, stands on a hillock on the far west side of the estate. The central dairymaid's cottage is flanked by two smaller buildings. One contains a tiled

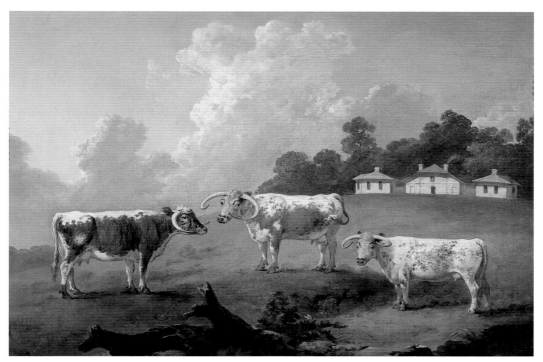

Oil painting of 1797 by Julius Caesar Ibbetson showing three of Lord Mansfield's long-horned Warwickshire cattle standing in front of the dairy buildings. This was one of three portraits of cattle painted by Ibbetson for Lady Mansfield

octagonal room with a cooling fountain in the centre and an ice-house beneath. The other had a room for making butter, with a china closet for Lady Mansfield's porcelain, and an ornamental tea-room where Louisa and her successors could entertain guests.

Inside the house the Mansfields employed the artist Julius Caesar Ibbetson to decorate their new Music Room (which faced towards the dairy) with scenes showing types of agriculture, fancifully represented as being performed by naked children. It was doubtless through Louisa's influence that Ibbetson came to Kenwood, as he had former connections with her family. In 1787 her younger brother Charles Cathcart had employed Ibbetson as the draughtsman on a British embassy to Peking. Charles died before reaching China, and Ibbetson returned to England unpaid. A few years later Louisa's cousin Robert Greville took the artist on a tour of north Wales and some of the resulting sketches of the Welsh landscape were subsequently incorporated into the friezes for the Music Room.

These were difficult years for Ibbetson, both personally and financially, and he may not have finished the decorative scheme as intended: in any case, the second Earl died in 1796 and never saw the work completed.

In September 1797 a new Lady Mansfield arrived as wife of the third Earl, Louisa's son. The following month Louisa married her devoted cousin Robert Greville. She remained Countess of Mansfield in her own right, but her influence at Kenwood must have waned gradually as a new generation took over.

The largest painting in Ibbetson's scheme for the Music Room represents a group of winged cherubs playing instruments on a golden cloud, which appeared to float out of the organ

The Third Earl and Royal Guests

David William Murray succeeded his father as third Earl in 1796 when he was nineteen. He appears to have held no ambitions for public office but as a patron of artists, architects, decorators and landscape gardeners he was clearly a Regency gentleman of taste. Among artists he commissioned works from Stubbs, Hoppner, Wilkie and Linnell. He also collected Old Master paintings, French furniture and porcelain.

The third Earl continued the landscape improvements begun by his father and added further land to the estate from adjacent gardens on the east and west sides. He engaged William Atkinson, a former pupil of the then leading architect, James Wyatt, to make numerous improvements. Atkinson's first work at Kenwood (and his first known work anywhere) was a picturesque Hermitage built in 1803; he went on to redecorate the house completely in 1815–17. At the same time, as architect to the Board of Ordnance, Atkinson designed a prefabricated house to be erected on St Helena for the exiled Napoleon Bonaparte, and he provided the same stencilled pattern for the Dining Room walls at Kenwood as for Bonaparte's house. Between 1803 and 1812 he rebuilt Scone Palace, Perthshire, which the Earl had inherited, and this led to the commission to build Abbotsford, Roxburghshire, the country house of Sir Walter Scott.

The third Earl also commissioned work from the fashionable upholsterers and cabinet-makers of the day, such as Tatham and Bayley and Nicholas Morel, who supplied furnishings to the Prince of Wales, later George IV, at Carlton House and Windsor Castle.

In 1818 Grand Duke Michael Pavlovich, grandson of Catherine the Great and brother of Tsars Alexander I and Nicholas I, visited Scone Palace and Kenwood. On 23 July 1835 King William IV and Queen Adelaide paid a visit and dined at Kenwood. Three years later the landscape architect John Claudius Loudon described Kenwood in his *Suburban Gardener and Villa Companion* as 'beyond all question, the finest country residence in the suburbs of London, in point of natural beauty of the ground and wood, as in point also of the main features of art'.

The Later Earls

In 1840 William David Murray (1806–98) succeeded his father as fourth Earl. Three years later he held a grand *fête champêtre* at Kenwood, with Prince Albert among the guests of honour. Generally he preferred Scone Palace, however, and spent only three months of each year at Kenwood. In 1889 he sold off 201 acres (81ha) to form an extension to Hampstead Heath. Nine years later his grandson and namesake inherited the title, but in 1906 the fifth Earl – 'the most eligible bachelor in London' – died suddenly. His brother, the sixth Earl, followed their father's and grandfather's examples in preferring to be at Scone, and Kenwood ended its days as a family home by being let to tenants.

Grand Duke Michael

One of the most dashing characters in Kenwood's history, Grand Duke Michael Michaelovitch (1861–1929), signed a twenty-one-year lease on the furnished house and moved in with his wife and three children in 1910. Grandson of Tsar Nicholas I and second cousin of Nicholas II, he had become a Lieutenant-Colonel in the Caucasian Sharpshooters and a Chevalier of the Black Eagle before being exiled from Russia in 1891 for marrying beneath his aristocratic rank. Sophie, Countess of Merenberg, was the grand-daughter of the poet Pushkin. She was not allowed to assume Grand Ducal rank, but was given the inferior title of Countess Torby. The couple became 'the uncrowned king and queen of Cannes society' where the exiled Grand Duke became President of the Cannes Golf Club (complete with customised lengthened clubs as he was over 6ft 6in or 2m tall). Here he met a fellow golfer, Arthur Crosfield, the soap magnate who had built 'Witanhurst', the largest private house in London after Buckingham Palace. Witanhurst overlooks the Kenwood estate and Crosfield must have introduced the Grand Duke to his neighbour as a suitable tenant as part of his campaign to save the rural outlook from his home. (A plaque commemorating Crosfield's involvement may be seen on the terrace.) Before moving in to Kenwood, Grand Duke Michael had the meadow between Kenwood and Parliament Hill converted into a golf course.

The Grand Duke and his wife lived in style with 'big dogs and even bigger Circassian guards in glamorous uniforms patrolling the grounds'. In 1913 *Country Life* devoted a feature article to their home at Kenwood, which now served as a suitable setting in which to launch their débutante daughters on society. In 1916 Countess Nada married Prince George of Battenberg (elder brother of Earl Mountbatten of Burma and uncle of Prince Philip) and the following year Countess Zia married the diamond heir Harold Wernher (later Sir Harold Wernher of Luton Hoo). That same year the Grand Duke lost his brother, and his fortune, in

the Russian Revolution. With his income reduced, he surrendered the remaining fourteen years of his lease and moved out of Kenwood with his wife and their son, Count Michael Torby, to Cambridge Gate, Regent's Park. Their heir died unmarried in 1959 after a career in fashion and theatre set design and was buried with his parents in Hampstead Cemetery, Fortune Green Road.

The Music Room around 1913, when the house was let to Grand Duke Michael, whose portrait by Galeoto can be seen in the background

The Upper Hall in 1913, with portraits from the Mansfield family's collection. These survive today at their Scottish seat, Scone Palace, Perthshire

An American Millionairess

The Mansfields' last private tenant at Kenwood was Nancy Leeds, the widow of an American tin-plate manufacturer who had left her £8 million. After leaving Kenwood Mrs Leeds married Prince Christopher of Greece in 1920. Her son, William B Leeds Jnr ('The Tin Plate Croesus'), married Grand Duke Michael's niece, Princess Xenia in 1922.

Grand Duke Michael with his daughters Nada and Zia, and son Michael

'Save Kenwood' *poster by the cartoonist 'Poy' (Percy Fearon), 1921, for the Kenwood Preservation Council*

RIGHT Edward Cecil Guinness, first Earl of Iveagh, *painted by H M Paget after Sir A S Cope around 1912, shows him in the ball-dress uniform of an Honorary Lieutenant, Royal Naval Reserve, with the sash and star of the Order of St Patrick*

OPPOSITE *Above the Music Room door hangs a fragment of the original decorative scheme by Julius Caesar Ibbetson*

The Saving of Kenwood

By 1910 the sixth Earl had decided to sell Kenwood to developers, partly owing to the Government's introduction of death duties. The plans were shelved when war broke out but were revived in a modified form in the 1920s.

From 1918 Arthur Crosfield led a series of public campaigns to save the estate. An appeal launched in 1921 failed to raise sufficient funds to buy the estate for the public and in November 1922 the contents of the house were sold at auction and the land was pegged out as building plots. Between December 1922 and 1924, 132 acres (53.5ha) were saved by the appeal and were opened to the public in 1925.

On 31 December 1924 Edward Cecil Guinness, first Earl of Iveagh, took a ten-year lease on the house and a fortnight later his family trust bought the freehold of the house and remaining 74 acres (30ha). Iveagh must have been well aware of the campaign to save Kenwood as in 1900 he had purchased two houses on the edge of Hampstead Heath for his own use: Heath House and Heathlands. In that year he had also publicly opposed plans by the Hampstead and Charing Cross Railway to develop a railway station and hotel at White Stone Pond overlooking the Heath.

Following his death in 1927, the house and park opened to the public in 1928.

The First Earl of Iveagh

Edward Cecil Guinness, first Earl of Iveagh, formed the most important collection of Old Master paintings to be given to the nation in the twentieth century. His great-grandfather, Arthur Guinness, had founded the Guinness brewery in Dublin in 1759. Edward Cecil, the youngest of three brothers, entered the family business as an apprentice when he was fifteen. In 1876, aged twenty-eight, he bought out his brothers' shares and over the next ten years he multiplied the business's value five-fold. In 1886 the family brewery became a public company and Edward Cecil retired, a millionaire at thirty-eight.

In Ireland he is best known for continuing the family tradition of philanthropy, particularly for his donations to establish trusts for workers' dwellings, in recognition of which he was

created a baronet in 1885, and was elevated to the peerage as Baron Iveagh in 1891. In 1909, on the personal recommendation of King Edward VII, he became Viscount Iveagh and in 1919 he received his earldom.

In England, however, he is best known as a collector. All but one of the paintings he bequeathed along with Kenwood were purchased from the dealers Agnew's. One of the legends of Bond Street tells how (on 23 June 1887) this quiet and reserved man first entered a different gallery, but on finding the partners out to lunch he crossed the road to Agnew's. Here the partners were also absent but an enterprising sales assistant risked showing him some of the best pictures reserved for major clients. He bought two on the spot, and over the next four years purchased a further 240 paintings, drawings and portrait miniatures from Agnew's to furnish his vast town house, 4 and 5 Grosvenor Place.

But for Lord Iveagh, many of the paintings at Kenwood would now be in North American collections. He purchased the most fashionable names in art, equivalent to buying paintings by Van Gogh, Monet or Picasso today, just before the great American collectors of the 'Gilded Age' entered the market. At Kenwood there are masterpieces by seventeenth-century Dutch and Flemish painters, most notably Rembrandt, Vermeer, Hals, Van Dyck, Snyders and Cuyp.

The Flower Gatherers *from the studio of François Boucher (1703–70) was the first painting Lord Iveagh purchased from the Bond Street dealers Agnew's, through whom he formed most of his collection*

These are complemented by works by their eighteenth- and early nineteenth-century British admirers: there are sixteen paintings by Reynolds, seven by Gainsborough, six by Romney, two by Raeburn, along with paintings by Lawrence, Turner, Landseer and a group of French Rococo scenes by Boucher and Pater. The closest equivalents to The Iveagh Bequest, Kenwood today in terms of period taste are two American house museums: The Frick Collection in New York (opened in 1931) and The Huntington Library and Art Gallery in San Marino, California (opened in 1927).

In England, Iveagh was probably inspired by the Wallace Collection in London (opened in 1900) and The Lady Lever Art Gallery at Port Sunlight, Liverpool (opened in 1922). Kenwood provides the opportunity to appreciate the paintings in various ways: in an historic house setting; in terms of the influence of Dutch and Flemish painters on British art; and as examples of the taste of a late Victorian collector.

The Iveagh Bequest

In 1929 an Act of Parliament was passed specifically to safeguard Kenwood House, the 74 acres (30ha) of land in Lord Iveagh's bequest and the art collection. It also endorsed 'the first Lord Iveagh's wishes that the atmosphere of a gentleman's private park should be preserved'. The Iveagh Bequest Act gave control to six Administrative Trustees, four of whom were nominees of the Guinness family; the other two were a representative of the London County Council and the Director of the National Gallery. Since 1986 English Heritage has been Sole Administrative Trustee of the Iveagh Bequest, Kenwood. In recent years it has carried out extensive repairs to the designed landscape, has undertaken the most substantial redecoration of the interior since it first opened to the public in 1928, has added to the collection of furniture and paintings, and has organised scholarly exhibitions on British art and collecting.

Further Reading

Gene Adams, 'Dido Elizabeth Belle. A Black Girl at Kenwood', *Camden History Review*, 12 (1984), pp 10–14

Julius Bryant, *Finest Prospects: Three Historic Houses*, exhibition catalogue (Kenwood, 1986)

Julius Bryant, *Robert Adam: Architect of Genius* (London, 1992)

Julius Bryant, *London's Country House Collections* (London, 1993)

Julius Bryant, 'Villa Views and the Uninvited Audience' in *The Georgian Villa*, ed. D Arnold (Stroud, 1996) pp 11–24

Julius Bryant and Carol Colson, *The Landscape of Kenwood* (London, 1990)

John Carswell, *The Saving of Kenwood and the Northern Heights* (Henley on Thames, 1992)

Stephen Daniels, *Humphry Repton* (New Haven & London, 1999)

Sebastian Edwards *et al*, *Miniatures at Kenwood. The Draper Gift* (London, 1997)

Anne French (ed.), *The Earl and Countess Howe by Gainsborough*, exhibition catalogue (Kenwood, 1988)

Edmund Heward, *Lord Mansfield* (London, 1979)

Jacob Simon, 'Humphry Repton at Kenwood: A Missing Red Book', *Camden History Review*, 11 (1984), pp 4–9

For further references, including historic sources, see the previous guidebook by Julius Bryant, *The Iveagh Bequest, Kenwood* (London, 1990)